PHERAS & PRIORITIES

NAVIGATING MODERN MARRIAGE WITH ANCIENT WISDOM

JAY ARIWALA

Contents

PREFACE

This book is a culmination of love, support, and inspiration from many individuals. I am deeply grateful to my parents, whose unwavering love and belief in me have been the guiding light of my life. Their constant encouragement and support have made this book possible.

I am also immensely thankful to my friends and family, who have shared their experiences and insights, enriching the narrative with real-life lessons in love and relationships. Their stories and perspectives have added depth and authenticity to the book.

Special thanks to my mentors and teachers, who have nurtured my passion for writing and provided invaluable guidance throughout this journey. Their wisdom and expertise have helped me shape this book into what it is today.

And finally, to all the readers who have chosen to embark on this journey with me, thank you for your time and attention. I hope this book resonates with you and offers insights that enrich your own relationships. May you find love, understanding, and happiness in your journey together.

Prologue

In the bustling city of Delhi, amidst the cacophony of life, a young couple, Raj and Anika, embarked on their journey of marriage. Raj, a hardworking and talented software engineer, and Anika, a lively and expressive artist, found love in each other's contrasting worlds. Their love story, much like any other, was filled with dreams and promises. Little did they know, their path would soon be lined with the trials and tribulations that test the mettle of any marriage.

Raj was the kind of person who thrived on structure and order. His days were meticulously planned, and his dedication to his career was evident in every project he undertook. Colleagues admired him for his discipline and his ability to solve complex problems with ease. But behind his professional success was a man who valued family and cherished the idea of building a life with someone he loved deeply.

Anika, on the other hand, was a free spirit. Her days were unpredictable, often dictated by bursts of creative inspiration. She painted her emotions, pouring her heart and soul onto canvases that adorned her small gallery. Friends admired her for her passion and the way she saw beauty in the world around her. Yet, behind her vibrant personality was a woman who longed for stability and a partner who would support her dreams.

Their love story began in a way that seemed straight out of a movie. They met at a mutual friend's wedding, where Raj was instantly captivated by Anika's laughter and Anika was drawn to Raj's quiet confidence. They spent the evening talking, discovering how their different worlds complemented each other perfectly. Over time, their bond grew stronger, leading them to the decision to marry.

The wedding was a grand affair, celebrated with the typical exuberance of Indian weddings. Friends and family gathered, showering the couple with blessings and love. Raj and Anika were the picture of happiness, dancing and laughing, their eyes filled with dreams of a shared future. But as the wedding festivities ended and real life began, they quickly realized that marriage required more than just love and dreams.

Raj's parents, Vikram and Meera, had spent over four decades together, navigating the ups and downs of life. They had grown wise with experience, understanding the nuances of marriage that their son and daughter-in-law were yet to discover. Vikram and Meera's relationship was a testament to the power of patience, compromise, and unwavering support.

Vikram, a retired school principal, was a man of few words but deep wisdom. His calm demeanor and thoughtful insights had guided many students through their formative years. Meera, a former teacher and now a community volunteer, was known for her warmth and ability to make everyone feel valued. Together, they had weathered many storms and celebrated countless joys, always finding strength in each other.

With a deep sense of responsibility, Vikram and Meera took it upon themselves to guide Raj and Anika through the early challenges of their married life. They understood that while love was the foundation, a successful marriage requires much more. They introduced Raj and Anika to the timeless wisdom found in the CSA Model.

The CSA Model was something Vikram and Meera had developed over their years together. It wasn't a formal theory but rather a practical approach to maintaining a healthy and loving relationship.

Raj and Anika were eager to learn from his parents Vikram and Meera's experience. They knew that the wisdom imparted by Raj's parents would be invaluable as they navigated the complexities of married life. The journey ahead was sure to be filled with challenges, but with the guidance of Vikram and Meera, they felt confident that they could build a strong and lasting relationship.

As they embarked on this new chapter of their lives, Raj and Anika understood that their love story was just beginning. The lessons they would learn and the experiences they would share would shape their marriage and help them grow as individuals and as a couple. With love as their foundation and the CSA Model as their guide, they were ready to face whatever life had in store for them.

I

Destined Meeting

In the bustling city of Delhi, where tradition and modernity seamlessly blend, a chance meeting at a mutual friend's wedding would forever change the lives of Raj and Anika. Raj, a passionate software engineer with a cool-headed approach, went to the wedding as a sign of respect for his childhood buddy. Anika, a vibrant and passionate artist, was present to encourage her closest friend, the bride. Little did they know, this event would mark the beginning of their love story.

The wedding was a grand celebration, filled with vibrant colors, melodious music, and joyous laughter. Raj stood on the sidelines, observing the festivities with a serene smile, when he heard the most captivating sound: Anika's laughter. Her laughter was infectious, and it drew Raj's attention like a magnet.

Anika, meanwhile, was bustling around, ensuring everything was perfect for her friend's big day. As she moved through the crowd, her eyes met Raj's, and she was struck by his quiet confidence. Intrigued by his calm presence amidst the chaos, she decided to introduce herself.

"Hi, I'm Anika. You must be Raj, the groom's friend?" she asked with a warm smile.

Raj nodded, his interest piqued. "Yes, that's right. It's nice to meet you, Anika."

As the evening progressed, Raj and Anika found themselves gravitating towards each other. They began to talk, discovering how their different worlds complemented each other perfectly. Raj admired Anika's passion for art and her ability to find beauty in everything around her. Anika, in turn, was fascinated by Raj's dedication to his career and his thoughtful perspective on life.

They spent the evening in deep conversation, sharing their dreams, aspirations, and stories from their past. Raj was captivated by Anika's creativity and zest for life, while Anika was drawn to Raj's intelligence and gentle nature. Their connection was undeniable, and by the end of the night, they felt as if they had known each other for years.

Over the following months, Raj and Anika's bond grew stronger. They spent time exploring Delhi together, from its bustling markets to its serene temples. They supported each other's passions, with Raj attending Anika's art exhibitions and Anika learning about the latest advancements in Raj's software projects. Their relationship blossomed, built on a foundation of mutual respect and admiration.

One evening, while they were strolling through Lodhi Gardens, Raj decided it was time to take their relationship to the next level. He had planned a special surprise for Anika, something that reflected their unique bond.

As they walked hand in hand, Raj led Anika to a beautifully decorated gazebo. Inside, fairy lights twinkled, and Anika's favorite flowers adorned the space. An easel stood in the center with a blank canvas, and beside it, a small table held a paint palette and brushes.

"Raj, what is all this?" Anika asked, her eyes wide with surprise and delight.

Raj smiled, taking her hands in his. "Anika, you've brought so much color and joy into my life. I wanted to create a moment that reflects our journey together. I want us to paint our future together, starting with this blank canvas."

Anika's eyes filled with tears of happiness as Raj knelt down and pulled out a small box from his pocket. "Anika, will you marry me and be my partner in this beautiful journey called life?"

Overwhelmed with emotion, Anika nodded. "Yes, Raj! I can't imagine my life without you."

With their engagement, Raj and Anika's families were brought together to celebrate their union. Both families were delighted and wholeheartedly supported their decision. Raj's parents, Vikram and Meera, were especially pleased to see their son so happy. They welcomed Anika with open arms, appreciating her warm personality and the love she had for their son.

Anika's parents were equally thrilled. They admired Raj's respect for their daughter's independence and his genuine affection for her. The families came together to plan the wedding, eager to celebrate the love and commitment of Raj and Anika.

The preparations for the wedding were a blend of tradition and modernity, reflecting Raj and Anika's unique personalities. Anika's artistic touch was evident in the décor, while Raj's meticulous planning ensured everything went smoothly. Friends and family from both sides pitched in, adding their own touches to make the day special.

As the wedding day approached, the excitement grew. Raj and Anika were ready to embark on this new chapter of their lives, confident in the strength of their bond and the support of their families.

Their love story, which began with a chance meeting at a wedding, had come full circle. They were about to step into a future filled with promise, love, and the inevitable challenges that they were prepared to face together.

Thus began their journey, with a foundation built on mutual respect, love, and the timeless wisdom of their parents. The stage was set for Raj and Anika's grand wedding, a celebration of their love and commitment to each other.

II
Tying the Knot

The day dawned bright and clear, the kind of perfect day that seemed tailor-made for a wedding. Raj and Anika's families had gathered in the sprawling garden of a grand hotel in Jaipur, the city of palaces and royal heritage. The venue was decorated with vibrant marigold flowers, shimmering drapes, and twinkling fairy lights. Every corner was filled with joy and excitement as family and friends mingled, waiting for the ceremony to begin.

Anika, dressed in a stunning red bridal lehenga, adorned with intricate gold embroidery, looked like a princess from a fairy tale. Her jewelry sparkled, and her face glowed with happiness and anticipation. Her friends and cousins fussed over her, making sure every detail was perfect. She felt a mix of emotions—excitement, nervousness, and a deep sense of joy.

Raj, in a regal sherwani, embroidered in gold and paired with a traditional turban, waited eagerly at the mandap (wedding altar). He looked around at the familiar faces, feeling a sense of pride and contentment. His best friends stood by his side, sharing jokes and lightening the mood.

As the ceremony began, the sacred fire crackled at the center of the mandap, surrounded by the chanting of mantras by the priest. Raj and Anika performed the rituals, their hands joined, promising to be with each other through every joy and sorrow. They exchanged garlands, symbolizing their acceptance of each other as life partners.

When it came time for the vows, both Raj and Anika felt a profound sense of connection. They promised to support each other, to share their dreams, and to face all challenges together. As they circled the fire, each step felt like a solid affirmation of their commitment to each other.

After the ceremony, the celebrations continued with a grand reception. The garden was transformed into a festive wonderland with tables laden with delicious food, a live band playing romantic tunes, and a dance floor where guests were already moving to the rhythm of the music.

Raj and Anika made their grand entrance as husband and wife, greeted by cheers and applause. They moved from table to table, thanking their guests for being part of their special day. The happiness and love in the air were palpable.

The couple shared their first dance, swaying to a beautiful melody that spoke of love and promises. Anika rested her head on Raj's shoulder, feeling safe and loved. Raj held her close, knowing that this moment marked the beginning of their new life together.

As the night progressed, the dance floor filled with friends and family, everyone celebrating the union of two souls. Laughter, music, and the clinking of glasses echoed through the garden. Raj and Anika couldn't stop smiling, their hearts full of joy and anticipation for the future.

Amidst the festivities, there were small moments that hinted at future challenges. After the ceremony, as they sat down for dinner, Anika noticed Raj was a bit distracted. He was constantly checking his phone, responding to messages from work. She felt a twinge of irritation but brushed it off, reminding herself that today was a celebration.

Later, as they mingled with the guests, Anika's aunt cornered Raj. "Beta, now that you're married, when can we expect some good news?" she asked with a mischievous glint in her eye.

Raj laughed it off, but Anika noticed a flicker of discomfort. They had talked about taking time before starting a family, focusing on their careers and enjoying their time together as a couple. She made a mental note to discuss this with Raj later, ensuring they were both on the same page about their plans.

Another small conflict arose when they were taking family photos. Raj's mother insisted on multiple retakes, wanting the perfect picture, while Anika's feet were aching from standing in her heavy bridal attire. Anika tried to hide her discomfort, but Raj noticed and suggested taking a break. His mother frowned, not pleased with the interruption.

These minor disagreements didn't overshadow the joy of the day, but they were small signs of the adjustments and compromises that lay ahead. Raj and Anika were excited about their future but realized that blending their lives and families would come with its own set of challenges.

As the night came to an end, Raj and Anika found a quiet moment to themselves. They sat on a swing in the garden, away from the noise and the crowd. Anika leaned against Raj, feeling the weight of the day's events finally sinking in.

"Today was perfect," Anika whispered, looking up at the starry sky.

Raj kissed her forehead. "Yes, it was. And it's just the beginning, Anika. We have so much to look forward to."

They talked about their dreams and plans, their hopes for the future, and the life they wanted to build together. They acknowledged that while there would be challenges, their love and commitment would help them navigate through anything.

That night, as they lay in each other's arms, Raj and Anika felt a deep sense of contentment. Their wedding day had been a beautiful celebration of their love, surrounded by the people who mattered most to them. They knew that the journey ahead would be filled with ups and downs, but they were ready to face it together, hand in hand.

As they drifted off to sleep, they held onto the promise they had made to each other—to love, to support, and to cherish one another, no matter what life brought their way.

III

The First Challenge

The honeymoon phase was wonderful, filled with joy and excitement. Raj and Anika returned from their honeymoon in Bali, feeling closer than ever. However, the reality of daily life soon began to settle in, bringing with it new challenges.

One evening, a few weeks after their return, Anika was preparing dinner while Raj was in the living room, engrossed in a work call. Anika had planned a special meal to celebrate their first month of marriage. She had spent hours in the kitchen, trying out a new recipe she thought Raj would love.

As the dinner time approached, Anika called out to Raj, "Dinner is ready! Come and eat before it gets cold."

"Just a minute, Anika," Raj replied, still focused on his call.

Anika waited for a few more minutes, but when Raj didn't show up, she felt a wave of frustration. She walked into the living room and saw Raj deeply engrossed in his laptop, still talking on the phone.

"Raj, I've been waiting for you," Anika said, trying to keep her voice calm. "Dinner is getting cold."

Raj looked up, a bit startled. "I'm sorry, Anika. This call is important. I'll be there as soon as I'm done."

Anika felt her patience wearing thin. "I understand work is important, but I spent a lot of time making dinner. Can't it wait for just a little while?"

Raj sighed. "I know, but this is urgent. I promise I'll be quick."

Anika nodded and went back to the dining table, but the initial excitement of the evening had faded. By the time Raj finally joined her, the food was cold, and Anika was visibly upset.

"I'm really sorry, Anika," Raj said, reaching for her hand. "I didn't mean to make you wait."

"I get that work is important, Raj, but I feel like you're always busy," Anika replied, her voice tinged with disappointment. "It's like you don't have time for us anymore."

Raj felt a pang of guilt. "I didn't realize it was bothering you so much. Work has been demanding lately, but I'll try to be more mindful."

Anika appreciated his apology, but the issue lingered. This incident highlighted a growing concern—Raj's work often took precedence, leaving Anika feeling neglected. They both knew this was something they needed to address to prevent further strain on their relationship.

The weekend following their argument, Raj and Anika visited Raj's parents for a family gathering. Raj's parents lived in a spacious house in South Delhi, where they frequently hosted family events. The house was buzzing with activity, filled with the laughter and chatter of relatives catching up.

Anika and Raj tried to put on a happy face, but the tension between them was noticeable. Raj's mother, Meera, had a keen eye for such things. She noticed Anika's subdued demeanor and Raj's attempts to bridge the gap.

During a quiet moment in the kitchen, while helping Anika with the tea, Meera gently asked, "Is everything alright, beta? You seem a bit off today."

Anika hesitated, not wanting to burden her mother-in-law with their issues, but she also felt the need to talk. "It's just... Raj has been very busy with work lately, and I feel like we don't spend enough time together. I know it's important, but it's been hard."

Meera nodded understandingly. "It's normal to have these challenges early on. Balancing work and personal life can be tricky. Have you talked to Raj about how you feel?"

"Yes, we did," Anika replied. "He apologized, but I still feel worried. I don't want this to become a pattern."

Meera smiled reassuringly. "Communication is key, Anika. You both need to find a balance that works for you. And it's okay to remind Raj when you need his time and attention."

Meanwhile, in the living room, Raj's father, Vikram, noticed his son's preoccupation. He pulled Raj aside and asked, "Is everything okay with you and Anika? You both seem a bit distant today."

Raj sighed, feeling the weight of his father's concern. "We had a small argument about my work. Anika feels I'm not spending enough time with her. I didn't realize how much it was affecting her."

Vikram placed a hand on Raj's shoulder. "Son, marriage requires constant effort from both sides. Your work is important, but so is your relationship with Anika. Make sure you're giving her the time and attention she needs."

Raj nodded, appreciating his father's advice. "I'll do better, Dad. I don't want her to feel neglected."

The rest of the day went smoothly, with Raj and Anika trying their best to enjoy the family gathering. However, the conversation with Raj's parents had given them both valuable insights. They realized the importance of maintaining a balance and the need for open communication to keep their relationship strong.

That evening, after returning home, Raj and Anika sat down to talk. "I talked to your mom today," Anika began. "She gave me some good advice about balancing our time."

Raj nodded. "I spoke to my dad too. He reminded me that I need to make sure you don't feel neglected. I'm really sorry, Anika. I'll try to be more present." Anika smiled, feeling hopeful. "Thank you, Raj. I know work is important, but our relationship is too. Let's find a way to make it work."

They decided to set some ground rules: dedicating certain evenings to each other without any work interruptions and ensuring they communicated more openly about their needs and expectations. It was a small but significant step towards resolving their conflict.

As they lay in bed that night, holding each other close, Raj and Anika felt a renewed sense of commitment. They knew that the road ahead would have its share of challenges, but they were ready to face them together. Their love was strong, and with a little effort and understanding, they could overcome anything that came their way.

The first major argument had taught them a valuable lesson about balance and communication. It was a reminder that while love formed the foundation of their relationship, maintaining it required ongoing effort and mutual respect. They fell asleep that night, comforted by the knowledge that they were in this together, ready to support and cherish each other through all the ups and downs of life.

IV

The CSA Model
Introduction

As the months went by, Raj and Anika continued to navigate the complexities of married life. Their relationship had its fair share of joys and challenges, but they were determined to make it work. During this time, they often sought advice and support from his parents, a couple who had been married for several years and seemed to have a solid understanding of maintaining a healthy relationship.

One evening, Raj and Anika invited his parent's over for dinner. After a delicious meal and some light-hearted conversation, the topic turned to relationships. Raj and Anika shared some of their recent struggles, including the balance between work and personal life.

Vikram nodded thoughtfully. "You know, when Meera and I got married, we faced similar challenges. That's when we came up with something we call the CSA Model. It stands for Compromise, Support, and Appreciation. It's really helped us maintain a strong and loving relationship."

Anika leaned forward, intrigued. "That sounds interesting. Can you tell us more about it?"

Meera smiled. "Of course. The CSA Model is all about ensuring that both partners feel valued and understood. Each part—Compromise, Support, and Appreciation—plays a crucial role. Let's start with Compromise."

To illustrate the concept of Compromise, they shared a personal story.

"A few years ago," Vikram began, "Meera and I were planning a vacation. I wanted to go to the mountains for some adventure sports, but Meera preferred a relaxing beach holiday. We were both really passionate about our choices and couldn't seem to agree."

Meera nodded, adding, "We realized that if we both stuck to our preferences without considering the other's feelings, it would lead to conflict and resentment. So, we decided to compromise. We split our vacation time—three days in the mountains and three days at the beach."

Raj and Anika listened intently, relating to the situation. Vikram continued, "This way, we both got to experience what we enjoyed, and it turned out to be one of our best vacations. We learned that compromise doesn't mean one person always has to give up their desires; it's about finding a middle ground where both partners feel satisfied."

Anika smiled. "That makes a lot of sense. It's about making sure both people feel heard and valued."

Meera agreed. "Exactly. Compromise is essential in any relationship. It shows that you respect your partner's needs and are willing to adjust for the sake of harmony. It can apply to various situations, whether it's choosing a vacation spot, deciding on household chores, or even picking a movie to watch."

Raj nodded thoughtfully. "We had a similar situation recently. Anika wanted to attend a family function, but I had a work event on the same day. We ended up feeling frustrated because neither of us wanted to miss our respective commitments. Maybe if we had thought about compromising, we could have found a solution that worked for both of us."

Vikram smiled. "That's the idea. It's about finding ways to meet each other halfway. Sometimes it means taking turns, sometimes it means combining plans, and sometimes it's just about understanding and flexibility."

Meera added, "The key is to communicate openly and honestly. Talk about what matters to you and why, and listen to your partner's perspective. When you approach situations with a willingness to compromise, it strengthens your bond and fosters mutual respect."

Anika felt a sense of relief. "I think incorporating the CSA Model could really help us. We've been struggling to balance our individual needs with our relationship, and compromise seems like a practical solution."

Raj agreed. "Absolutely. We should give it a try. It's about making small adjustments and understanding each other better."

Vikram and Meera exchanged a warm look. "We're glad to hear that," Vikram said. "Remember, the CSA Model isn't a one-time fix; it's a continuous process. Every situation is different, and the way you compromise will vary. The important thing is to keep the lines of communication open and to approach each challenge as a team."

Meera concluded, "And don't forget the other parts of the model—Support and Appreciation. We'll talk more about those next time. For now, focus on how you can incorporate compromise into your daily lives. It's a small step, but it can make a big difference."

Raj and Anika felt inspired by his parent's advice. They knew that implementing the CSA Model would require effort and patience, but they were committed to making their relationship work. That evening, as they lay in bed, they talked about the areas where they could start compromising and supporting each other better.

The introduction of the CSA Model marked a turning point for Raj and Anika. It provided them with a practical framework to navigate the challenges of married life, and they felt hopeful about the future. With Vikram and Meera's guidance, they were ready to embrace the journey of compromise, support, and appreciation, knowing that it would strengthen their bond and help them grow together.

V
Strength of Support

Raj and Anika had started to grasp the concept of compromise, understanding that marriage required meeting each other halfway. However, the next pillar of the CSA Model—Support—was just as crucial. Vikram and Meera knew that for Raj and Anika to truly thrive, they needed to learn how to support each other through life's challenges.

One evening, as the family sat together after dinner, Meera decided it was time to discuss the importance of support in marriage. "Raj, Anika, we've talked about compromise, but there's another aspect that's just as important—support. Being there for each other, especially during tough times, strengthens your bond and builds trust."

Raj nodded thoughtfully. "I understand, Mom. But can you give us an example of how you and Dad have supported each other?"

Vikram smiled. "Let me tell you about a challenging time in our lives."

Years ago, Vikram faced a significant setback in his career. As a school principal, he was respected and admired, but a sudden change in school management brought new policies and expectations that conflicted with his values. This situation caused Vikram immense stress and frustration, and he began to consider leaving his job.

"I remember those days vividly," Meera began. "Vikram would come home exhausted and disheartened. It pained me to see him like that, but I knew I had to be strong for both of us."

Meera decided to take action. She encouraged Vikram to talk about his feelings and frustrations, providing a listening ear without judgment. "I made sure he knew that I was there for him, no matter what decision he made," she explained. "We discussed his options, and I reminded him of his strengths and the positive impact he had on his students."

With Meera's unwavering support, Vikram found the courage to stand up for his principles. He approached the new management and voiced his concerns. Although it was a risky move, his honesty and integrity impressed them, and they decided to reconsider some of their policies.

"Your mother's support gave me the strength to face my fears," Vikram said. "Knowing she believed in me made all the difference."

Raj and Anika listened intently, reflecting on their own lives. Anika, in particular, felt a deep connection to the story. She had recently been struggling with a creative block, feeling uninspired and questioning her abilities as an artist. The pressure to succeed was overwhelming, and she often felt discouraged.

One night, Anika confided in Raj about her struggles. "I don't know if I'm cut out for this, Raj. What if I never create anything meaningful again?"

Raj took her hand, his eyes filled with empathy. "Anika, you are incredibly talented. I believe in you, even if you're doubting yourself right now. Let's work through this together."

Inspired by his parents' example, Raj decided to take action. He helped Anika set up a new studio space, free from distractions, and encouraged her to take breaks and find inspiration in different places. He attended art shows with her, giving her new ideas and perspectives.

Gradually, with Raj's support, Anika began to find her creative spark again. She started painting with renewed passion and confidence. "Raj's support meant everything to me," she later reflected. "Knowing he was there for me, no matter what, gave me the courage to keep going."

Raj and Anika realized that supporting each other was more than just being present; it was about actively participating in each other's lives and offering encouragement and assistance during tough times.

Vikram and Meera smiled, seeing the understanding dawning on the young couple's faces. "Remember," Meera said gently, "support is not just about solving each other's problems. It's about being a source of strength and encouragement. It's about showing your partner that you're in this together, no matter what."

Raj and Anika nodded, feeling more connected and prepared for the journey ahead. They knew that with compromise and support, they could face any challenge that came their way. The foundation of their marriage was growing stronger, brick by brick, as they learned from Vikram and Meera's wisdom and applied it to their own lives.

With this new understanding, Raj and Anika were ready to continue their journey, embracing the lessons of support and looking forward to the future with hope and determination.

VI

Essence of Appreciation

Having learned the importance of compromise and support, Raj and Anika were beginning to see the positive changes in their relationship. But Vikram and Meera knew that for their marriage to truly thrive, Raj and Anika needed to understand the third pillar of the CSA Model—Appreciation.

One evening, as the family gathered for their customary tea time, Vikram decided to introduce the concept of appreciation. "Raj, Anika, we've talked about compromise and support, but there's one more crucial element that binds a relationship together—appreciation. Recognizing and valuing each other's efforts, no matter how small, keeps the love and respect alive in a marriage."

Anika nodded thoughtfully. "I think I understand, but can you give us an example of how you and Mom show appreciation for each other?"

Meera smiled warmly. "Let me share a story from our early years."

In the early years of their marriage, Meera was a busy teacher, juggling work and household responsibilities. Despite her hectic schedule, she always made it a point to prepare Vikram's favorite meals, knowing how much he appreciated them.

"Your mother would wake up early every morning to make sure I had a hearty breakfast before heading to work," Vikram reminisced. "It wasn't just about the food; it was about the love and effort she put into it. I made sure to always thank her and let her know how much I valued those small gestures."

Meera continued, "And Vikram, despite his busy schedule as a principal, would always make time to help me with chores or surprise me with flowers, just to show that he appreciated everything I did. It made me feel loved and valued."

As Raj listened, he recalled a recent event at work. He had been working tirelessly on a project that led to his promotion. Anika had been his constant source of support, encouraging him and cheering him on. When he received the promotion, he realized he had not adequately shown his appreciation for her support.

"Anika, I've been so focused on my work that I forgot to thank you properly for all the support you've given me," Raj admitted. "I wouldn't have achieved this without you."

Anika smiled, her eyes shining with appreciation. "Raj, your hard work paid off, and I'm proud of you. But hearing you say that means a lot to me."

Raj decided to show his appreciation in a special way. He planned a surprise weekend getaway for Anika to one of her favorite places, where they could relax and spend quality time together. This gesture was not only a way to thank her but also to rekindle the romance in their relationship.

Meanwhile, Anika had been preparing for a solo exhibition at her art gallery. She had poured her heart and soul into her work, and the pressure was immense. Raj, inspired by his parents' example, made it a point to appreciate Anika's efforts every day.

"You're doing an amazing job, Anika. Your art is beautiful, and I'm sure the exhibition will be a huge success," Raj would tell her, making her feel valued and confident.

The night of the exhibition arrived, and Raj was there, beaming with pride as he saw Anika's artwork admired by so many. After the event, he took her out for a celebratory dinner, expressing how proud he was of her achievements.

"Your appreciation and support mean everything to me, Raj," Anika said, her eyes filled with gratitude. "Thank you for always being there for me."

Raj and Anika began to incorporate appreciation into their daily lives. They realized that it wasn't just about grand gestures but also about acknowledging the small things that often went unnoticed. A simple thank you, a word of encouragement, or a gesture of kindness went a long way in strengthening their bond.

Vikram and Meera watched with satisfaction as their children grew closer, their relationship fortified by the principles of the CSA Model. "Remember," Vikram advised, "appreciation is not just about what you do but how you make each other feel. It's about recognizing the effort and love that goes into every action."

Raj and Anika felt more in touch and ready for the road ahead. They were aware that they could overcome any obstacle if they were willing to make compromises, received encouragement, and were valued. The foundation of their marriage was becoming more solid than it had ever been.

With this fresh perspective, Raj and Anika were prepared to move on with their adventure, embracing the lessons of gratitude and eagerly anticipating what lay ahead.

VII
Power of Patience and Devotion

A few weeks after introducing Raj and Anika to the CSA Model, his parents invited them over for a cozy evening at their place. The setting was warm and inviting, with the aroma of freshly brewed chai filling the air. As they settled in with their cups of tea, the conversation turned to stories and traditions.

Meera, known for her love of hindu traditions and storytelling, decided to share a story that had always inspired her and Vikram in their marriage. "I want to tell you the story of Mahadev and Mata Parvati," she began. "It's a beautiful tale that highlights the power of patience and devotion in a relationship."

Raj and Anika listened eagerly as Meera started her tale.

"Mahadev, also known as Lord Shiva, is one of the principal deities in Hindu culture. He is the destroyer and creator of all things, a powerful and calm god. Mata Parvati, his consort, represents love, fertility, and devotion. Their union is often seen as the perfect balance of masculine and feminine energies."

Meera continued, "When Mata Parvati first met Lord Shiva, she was drawn to his intense and meditative nature. She fell deeply in love with him and decided that she wanted to marry him. However, Shiva was deeply engrossed in his ascetic practices and initially showed no interest in worldly matters, including marriage."

"Mata Parvati didn't give up," Meera said, her eyes shining with the passion of the story. "She undertook rigorous penance and severe austerities to win his affection. She meditated for years, showing immense patience and unwavering devotion. Her determination and love finally softened Lord Shiva's heart, and he accepted her as his wife."

"Mahadev and Mata Parvati's story teaches us that patience and devotion are key to overcoming obstacles in a relationship," Meera explained. "Despite the challenges and the time it took, Mata Parvati's love and patience eventually brought them together. Their union symbolizes the strength that comes from steadfastness and the deep bond that patience can create."

As Meera finished the story, Raj and Anika were deeply moved. They saw parallels in their own relationship, especially in how patience could play a crucial role in overcoming their challenges.

Anika was the first to speak. "I've always admired the story of Mahadev and Mata Parvati, but hearing it now makes me realize how much patience and devotion matter in a relationship. I think sometimes we forget that it's not just about solving problems quickly but also about being patient and giving each other time."

Raj nodded in agreement. "I can see how this applies to us. There are times when I get frustrated because I want things to change immediately. But maybe what we need is more patience and understanding."

Vikram added, "Patience doesn't mean doing nothing. It means being present, understanding your partner's perspective, and waiting with a positive mindset. It's about trusting the process and believing that with time and effort, things will improve."

Meera smiled, "Exactly. Patience allows you to be more compassionate and empathetic. It helps you to stay calm during conflicts and gives you the strength to support each other through difficult times."

Anika thought about their recent argument over Raj's work commitments. "I think I need to be more patient when it comes to Raj's work. I know he's trying his best, and I need to give him the space and time to balance everything."

Raj squeezed her hand. "And I need to be more patient with you, Anika. Sometimes I get so caught up in my work that I forget how it affects you. I promise to be more mindful and to make more time for us."

Meera shared another thought, "Devotion in a relationship is also about commitment and consistency. It's about showing your love and support every day, not just during the good times but especially during the challenging ones."

Vikram nodded, "Devotion means being there for each other, no matter what. It means showing up, even when things are tough, and reminding each other of the love that brought you together in the first place."

Raj and Anika left Vikram and Meera's home that evening feeling inspired and hopeful. They knew that incorporating patience and devotion into their relationship would require conscious effort, but they were ready to embrace this new approach.

In the following weeks, they made small but significant changes. Raj made a point to put his work aside during dinner, focusing entirely on Anika and their conversations. Anika, in turn, practiced patience by understanding the demands of Raj's job and not getting upset when he had to work late.

One evening, when Raj came home later than usual, he found Anika waiting for him with a warm smile and dinner ready. "I know you've had a long day," she said gently. "Let's eat and talk about it."

Raj felt a surge of gratitude. "Thank you for being so understanding, Anika. I really appreciate your patience."

Anika replied, "We're in this together, Raj. Just like Mahadev and Mata Parvati, we'll face our challenges with patience and devotion."

Their relationship gradually became stronger as they learned to navigate their differences with greater understanding and compassion. They realized that the power of patience lay in its ability to create a deeper bond, allowing them to support each other through thick and thin.

As they continued to grow together, Raj and Anika found that their love was becoming more resilient. They faced each challenge with renewed faith in each other, knowing that their patience and devotion would guide them through.

The story of Mahadev and Mata Parvati became a cornerstone of their relationship, reminding them that true love is not just about being together during the good times but also about standing by each other with patience and unwavering devotion, no matter what challenges life may bring.

VIII
Faith and Perseverance

Raj and Anika had been navigating their marriage with the principles of the CSA Model and the lessons from the story of Mahadev and Mata Parvati. Life was beginning to feel more balanced, and their relationship stronger. However, as with any journey, they soon encountered another test.

One evening, Raj received a call from his boss about an important business trip. It was a last-minute assignment that required Raj to travel abroad for a week. He knew this trip was crucial for his career, but he also understood that leaving on such short notice would be hard on Anika.

When he broke the news to her, Anika felt a pang of disappointment. "Another trip, Raj? We barely get any time together as it is," she said, trying to mask her sadness.

Raj took her hand. "I know, Anika. But this is really important for my job. It's just one week, and I'll be back before you know it."

Anika nodded, but her mind was filled with doubts. She trusted Raj, but the frequent separations were starting to take a toll. She worried about the strain it was putting on their relationship.

The week Raj was away felt like an eternity for Anika. She missed him terribly and found it hard to keep her worries at bay. She choose to spend a week at raj's parents house because she wanted to talk to Meera about the situation, and she began by explaining about the recent events that had occurred. She confided in Meera, who listened patiently.

"It's tough, Anika," Meera said. "I understand how you feel. But remember, faith in each other is essential. Raj loves you and is doing his best for both of you."

Anika sighed. "I know, but it's hard not to feel insecure. What if this keeps happening?"

Meera gave her a reassuring smile. "Let me share another story that might help. It's about Shri Ram and Mata Sita, and how their faith and perseverance helped them through the toughest times."

Meera began, "Shri Ram and Mata Sita's story is one of the most revered tales in Hindu culture. Shri Ram, the prince of Ayodhya, and Sita, the princess of Mithila, had a love that was pure and unwavering. Their journey was filled with trials, but their faith in each other remained steadfast."

"One of the most significant challenges they faced was during their exile. They were banished from the kingdom for fourteen years and had to live in the forest. Despite the harsh conditions, Mata Sita remained devoted to Shri Ram, and he to her. They supported each other through every hardship, their love and faith unwavering."

Meera continued, "However, their biggest test came when Mata Sita was abducted by the demon king Ravana. Shri Ram was devastated, but he never lost faith. He persevered, gathering an army of allies and embarking on a perilous journey to rescue her. Mata Sita, on the other hand, kept her faith in Shri Ram, believing that he would come for her no matter how long it took."

"After many trials and battles, Shri Ram defeated Ravana and rescued Mata Sita. Their reunion was a testament to their enduring love and faith in each other. They overcame the odds through perseverance and unwavering belief in their bond."

Meera looked at Anika. "The story of Shri Ram and Mata Sita teaches us that faith and perseverance are crucial in any relationship. No matter how difficult the situation, believing in each other and staying committed can help you overcome any challenge."

Anika found solace in Meera's words. She was reminded of the strength derived from steadfast faith and perseverance by the tale of Shri Ram and Mata Sita. She realized that while Raj's work commitments were challenging, her belief in their love needed to remain strong. She returned home before the day he was supposed to come.

When Raj returned from his trip, Anika welcomed him with open arms. "I missed you so much," she said, hugging him tightly.

Raj kissed her forehead. "I missed you too, Anika. I know it's not easy, but I appreciate your patience and understanding."

Anika smiled. "I've been thinking a lot while you were away. I want to focus on the faith we have in each other. No matter how tough things get, I believe we can get through it together."

Raj felt a surge of gratitude. "Thank you, Anika. I promise to make more time for us and to always prioritize our relationship."

They spent the evening talking and reconnecting, sharing their experiences from the past week. Anika's newfound perspective on faith and perseverance helped her approach their situation with a more positive outlook.

In the following months, Raj and Anika worked on strengthening their faith in each other. They communicated more openly about their concerns and reassured each other of their commitment. Raj made an effort to balance his work and personal life better, ensuring that Anika felt valued and supported.

One weekend, Raj surprised Anika with a trip to the mountains, a place they both loved. "I wanted to make up for the time I was away," he said. "Let's spend this weekend just focusing on us."

Anika's eyes lit up with joy. "This is perfect, Raj. Thank you."

As they hiked through the serene trails, surrounded by nature, Anika felt a deep sense of peace. She realized that their relationship was becoming stronger with each challenge they faced. The lessons from Shri Ram and Mata Sita's story had taught her the importance of holding steadfast to her beliefs and maintaining faith in their love.

Raj and Anika returned from their trip feeling rejuvenated and more connected than ever. They knew that life would continue to present challenges, but with faith and perseverance, they were ready to face them together.

The power of faith and perseverance in their marriage became a guiding principle for Raj and Anika. They learned that while external circumstances might be unpredictable, their inner strength and commitment to each other would always see them through. Their love, fortified by the lessons of patience, devotion, faith, and perseverance, was ready to stand the test of time.

IX

Sacrifice and Wisdom

Raj's career was thriving, thanks to his dedication and hard work. However, his success came with increased responsibilities and frequent travel. Anika, who had been supportive of Raj's career, found herself longing for more time with him. She also had her own aspirations and dreams that she had put on hold to support Raj.

One day, Raj received an offer for a significant promotion. It was a dream opportunity, but it required relocating to another city. The decision weighed heavily on both Raj and Anika. Moving would mean leaving behind their family, friends, and the comfortable life they had built together. Moreover, Anika would have to give up her art studio, which she loved and had worked hard to establish.

Raj was torn. He wanted to take the promotion but was worried about the impact it would have on Anika. "I don't want you to sacrifice your career and happiness for me," he told her one evening.

Anika smiled gently. "Raj, this is a huge opportunity for you. I can see how much it means to you. I want you to succeed and be happy. We'll find a way to make it work for both of us."

After much thought and discussion, Anika decided to close her art studio and move with Raj. It was a difficult decision, but she believed in their partnership and wanted to support Raj's ambitions.

The move was challenging, but Anika faced it with grace and resilience. She focused on creating a new home and finding ways to stay connected to her passions. She started volunteering and exploring new opportunities that the new city offered.

Raj was deeply appreciative of Anika's sacrifice. He made a conscious effort to balance his work commitments and ensure that Anika felt valued and supported. They knew that their journey was not just about individual successes but about growing and thriving together.

One evening, as they settled into their new home, Vikram and Meera visited to catch up and offer their support. The conversation naturally turned to the recent changes and challenges. Anika shared her feelings about the move and her hopes for the future.

Vikram listened thoughtfully. "Anika, your sacrifice for Raj is a beautiful example of selfless love. It reminds me of the story of Shri Krishn and Radha. Their love was profound and full of wisdom."

Raj and Anika were intrigued. They had always admired the tales of Shri Krishn and Radha but had never heard this particular story from Vikram's perspective.

Vikram began, "Shri Krishn and Radha's love is one of the most celebrated and revered in Hindu culture. Their relationship transcended the ordinary bounds of romance and became a symbol of divine love and spiritual connection."

"Radha and Shri Krishn's bond was incredibly deep, but their love was not bound by conventional norms. They understood and accepted each other completely. Radha's love for Shri Krishn was selfless and pure, and she was willing to make any sacrifice for his happiness."

"One of the most poignant aspects of their story is the wisdom that comes from such selfless love. Radha knew that her love for Krishn was eternal, even if circumstances separated them physically. She derived strength and wisdom from their spiritual connection, understanding that true love transcends physical presence and worldly desires."

Vikram continued, "Radha's wisdom teaches us that love is not just about being together all the time. It's about understanding, support, and selflessness. She sacrificed her own desires for the greater good, knowing that her love for Shri Krishn would always be a guiding light in her life."

Meera added, "Radha's love was rooted in deep wisdom and spirituality. She understood that sacrifices made out of love are not losses but acts of strength and devotion. This wisdom helps us navigate the complexities of relationships with grace and resilience."

Anika felt a profound connection to the story. "I see now that my sacrifice for Raj is not just about giving up something. It's about supporting each other's dreams and finding new ways to grow together. It's about the wisdom that comes from understanding and accepting each other's needs."

Raj took Anika's hand. "Anika, your support means the world to me. I promise to honor your sacrifice and ensure that we both find fulfillment in this new chapter of our lives."

Vikram smiled. "That's the essence of Radha and Shri Krishn's story. It's about mutual respect, understanding, and the wisdom that comes from selfless love. By supporting each other's dreams and making sacrifices when necessary, you strengthen your bond and create a deeper connection."

The story of Shri Krishn and Radha inspired Raj and Anika to embrace their new life with a renewed sense of purpose. Anika began exploring opportunities that aligned with her passions, while Raj made a conscious effort to ensure their relationship remained a priority.

As they navigated the challenges of their new life, they drew strength from the wisdom of Radha and Shri Krishn's love. They realized that their sacrifices were not just about giving up something but about gaining a deeper understanding of each other and their relationship.

In the months that followed, Raj and Anika found a new rhythm in their lives. Anika started a small business that allowed her to work from home and pursue her interests. Raj's career flourished, and he made sure to spend quality time with Anika, cherishing the moments they shared.

Their journey was not without challenges, but the wisdom they gained from the story of Radha and Krishn helped them navigate each obstacle with grace and resilience. They learned that true love is about more than just being together; it's about selflessness, understanding, and the wisdom that comes from supporting each other's dreams.

Raj and Anika's relationship grew stronger with each passing day. They knew that their love, fortified by the lessons of patience, devotion, faith, perseverance, sacrifice, and wisdom, would continue to guide them through life's challenges. Their journey together was a testament to the power of selfless love and the enduring strength of their bond.

X

Acceptance and Moving Forward

Raj and Anika had weathered many storms together, but they were about to face one of their biggest challenges yet. This conflict would test their ability to accept each other's flaws and differences.

The issue arose from a topic that had been a simmering tension in their relationship for some time: starting a family. Raj was eager to have children and felt it was the right time. Anika, however, was hesitant. She had just started her small business and wanted to focus on it before taking on the responsibilities of parenthood.

One evening, the topic came up again. Raj expressed his desire to start planning for a family. "Anika, I think we're ready. We've built a stable life, and I really want to have children soon," he said, his voice filled with anticipation.

Anika took a deep breath. "Raj, I understand how you feel, but I'm not ready yet. My business is still in its early stages, and I want to give it more time."

The discussion quickly turned heated. Raj felt that Anika was being dismissive of his feelings, while Anika felt pressured and unsupported. They both raised their voices, their frustration boiling over.

"You're always putting your career first!" Raj exclaimed. "When will it be the right time if it's never now?"

Anika, hurt by his words, shot back, "And you're not respecting my dreams! I need you to understand that I'm not ready. Why can't you see that?"

The argument ended with both of them feeling angry and misunderstood. They retreated to separate corners of their home, the silence between them heavy and painful.

The next day, Raj and Anika felt the weight of their unresolved conflict. They knew they needed to address it, but they were unsure how to start. Seeing the stress, Vikram and Meera provided advice because they would be living with them for a few more days.

"Raj, Anika, it's clear that this issue is very important to both of you," Vikram began. "It's time to put the CSA Model into practice fully. You need to find a way to Compromise, Support, and Appreciate each other's perspectives."

Meera added, "Acceptance is key here. You both have valid points, and it's essential to acknowledge each other's feelings. Let's work through this together."

Vikram suggested they start by finding a middle ground. "Raj, Anika isn't saying she never wants children. She's asking for more time. Anika, can you consider a timeline that you both can agree on?"

After some discussion, they agreed to revisit the idea in a year. This would give Anika the time she needed for her business while giving Raj a clear timeline to look forward to.

Meera emphasized the importance of mutual support. "Raj, show Anika that you support her dreams by being patient. Anika, reassure Raj that you do want a family and appreciate his eagerness."

Raj promised to support Anika's business by helping with marketing and networking, while Anika assured Raj that his desire for a family was important to her and that she was committed to finding the right balance.

Vikram and Meera also stressed the need for appreciation. "Regularly express gratitude for each other's efforts and sacrifices," Meera said. "It strengthens your bond."

Raj started acknowledging Anika's hard work and determination, while Anika expressed her appreciation for Raj's patience and support.

With the CSA Model in mind, Raj and Anika began to rebuild their connection again. They had open and honest conversations about their fears and hopes, creating a safe space for each other to express their feelings.

Anika shared her anxiety about balancing a business and a family. "I worry that I won't be able to give my best to either," she confided.

Raj, understanding her concerns, said, "I know it's a big responsibility, and I don't want to rush you. I just want us to plan our future together, when we're both ready."

They also made a conscious effort to spend quality time together, strengthening their emotional connection. They took long walks, cooked meals together, and had date nights, ensuring that their relationship remained a priority amidst their busy lives.

As the months passed, Anika's business flourished, and she felt more confident about the future. She appreciated Raj's unwavering support and patience, which made her love for him grow even deeper.

A year later, they revisited the conversation about starting a family. This time, the discussion was calm and understanding. Anika felt ready to take the next step, and Raj, having waited patiently, was more supportive than ever.

The journey had not been easy, but the conflict had brought them closer. They had learned the importance of acceptance and compromise, realizing that their love was strong enough to overcome any challenge.

Raj and Anika's relationship continued to thrive as they navigated the complexities of life together. They had embraced the CSA Model, finding ways to support and appreciate each other through every obstacle.

Their journey of acceptance and moving forward had taught them invaluable lessons. They understood that a successful relationship required ongoing effort, patience, and a willingness to grow together. With love, compromise, support, and appreciation as their guiding principles, Raj and Anika were assured of the depth of their relationship.

Reflections On The Journey

As the sun dipped below the horizon, casting long shadows across the garden, Raj and Anika sat on their porch, their hands intertwined. The gentle summer breeze carried the sweet scent of jasmine, filling the air with a sense of tranquility.

They had come a long way since their wedding day, navigating the challenges and joys of marriage with courage and determination. Their journey had been one of growth, understanding, and unwavering love.

Raj turned to Anika, his eyes reflecting the deep affection he felt for her. "I can't believe how far we've come," he said softly. "We've faced so much together, and our love has only grown stronger."

Anika smiled, her heart echoing his sentiments. "I remember when we first started dating, I was so unsure about the future. But now, looking back, I wouldn't change a thing."

They reminisced about the early days of their relationship, the stolen glances, the shared laughter, and the hesitant first steps towards commitment. They talked about the challenges they had overcome, the compromises they had made, and the lessons they had learned.

"Remember the time we had that big fight about whose family we would visit for Diwali?" Raj chuckled. "We were so stubborn, both insisting on our own way."

Anika laughed. "Yes, and then Dad and Mom stepped in and helped us see the bigger picture. They taught us the importance of compromise and finding solutions that work for both of us."

Their thoughts turned to Vikram and Meera, the wise parent's and loving couple who had guided them through the ups and downs of their marriage. Their support had been invaluable, their advice a beacon of light in times of darkness.

"I'm so grateful for Dad and Mom," Anika said. "They showed us that marriage is not just about love, but also about understanding, respect, and a willingness to grow together."

Raj nodded in agreement. "Their stories and wisdom have been a constant source of inspiration for us. They taught us that even the strongest relationships face challenges, but with love and commitment, we can overcome anything."

As they looked back on their journey, Raj and Anika realized how much they had evolved as individuals and as a couple. They had learned to communicate openly, to listen with empathy, and to support each other's dreams and aspirations.

"Marriage is a constant work in progress," Raj reflected. "It's about adapting, compromising, and finding new ways to connect with each other."

Anika added, "It's also about celebrating the small victories, cherishing the everyday moments, and appreciating the love that binds us together."

They knew that their journey was not over, that there would be more challenges and obstacles to overcome. But they also knew that they had the strength and resilience to face them together.

As the stars began to twinkle in the night sky, Raj and Anika held each other close, their hearts filled with gratitude and love. They had found their happily ever after, not in a fairy tale ending, but in the everyday moments of connection, the shared dreams, and the unwavering support that defined their marriage.

Their story was a testament to the power of love, the importance of communication, and the enduring strength of the human spirit. It was a story that would continue to unfold, chapter by chapter, as they navigated the beautiful and unpredictable journey of life together.